THE
INTERSECTION OF X AND Y

Poems by

Rebecca McClanahan

Copper Beech Press
Providence

Acknowledgment is made to the editors of these publications, where some of these poems, or earlier versions of them, first appeared: *Bellingham Review* ("Making Love to an Orphan"), *Boulevard* ("Traveling"), *The Georgia Review* ("X," "Pardon"), *The Gettysburg Review* ("Open Swim at the Y"), *G.W. Review* ("The Rooster"), *Indiana Review* ("Salvage"), *Kenyon Review* ("To the Absent Wife of the Beautiful Poet at the Writers' Conference," "This Side"), *Malahat Review* ("After the Miracle," "Interstate"), *New Virginia Review* ("Missionary"), *One Word Deep* ("Infant Hill, Elmwood Cemetery," "The Seed"), *Poetry* ("Sidekick," "Ex-Brother-in-Law," "Afterglow"), *Quarterly West* ("Demons," "First Husband"), *Southern Poetry Review* ("The Angle of Shadow, the Angle of Light"), and *The Southern Review* ("A Definition").

Special thanks to the North Carolina Arts Council, the MacDowell Colony, and Ashland University for fellowships and residencies during the years many of these poems were written. And ongoing gratitude to my friends, Cathy Smith Bowers, P.B. Newman, Jim Peterson, Diana Pinckney, Dede Wilson, and especially Gail Peck.—R.M.

Cover: "Skyla Caldwell and Joseph Curry," ©1996 by Lana Rubright.

Copyright© 1996 by Rebecca McClanahan
All rights reserved.
For information, address the publisher:
    Copper Beech Press
    English Department
    Box 1852
    Brown University
    Providence, Rhode Island 02912

Library of Congress Cataloging-in-Publication Data
McClanahan, Rebecca.
    The intersection of X and Y : poems / by Rebecca McClanahan.
    p. cm.
    ISBN 0-914278-70-3 (pbk. : alk. paper)
    I. Title.
PS3554.E9274I58   1996
811' .54—dc20   96-11192
                                                                  CIP

Set in Palatino by Louis Giardini
Printed and bound by McNaughton & Gunn
Manufactured in the United States of America
First Edition

*For Donald
and for my parents*

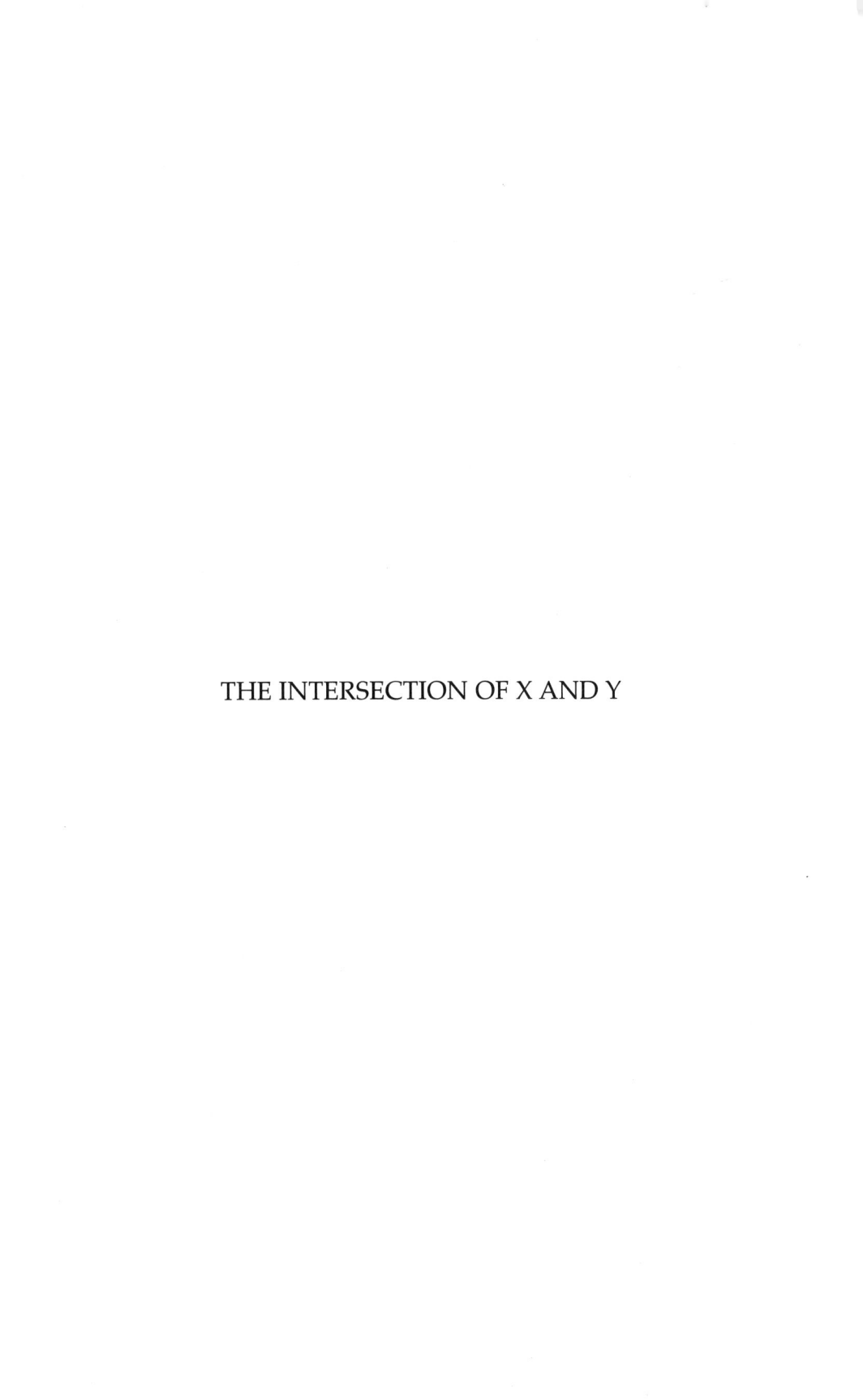

THE INTERSECTION OF X AND Y

Also by Rebecca McClanahan

Mother Tongue (University Press of Florida, 1987)
Mrs. Houdini (University Press of Florida, 1989)
One Word Deep: Lectures and Readings (Ashland Poetry Press, 1993)

A great truth is a truth whose opposite is also a great truth.

Christopher Morley

The smallest number, in the strict sense of the word "number," is two.

Aristotle

Contents

X	13
Sidekick	15
Traveling	17
Her Nakedness	19
Demons	20
The Angle of Shadow, the Angle of Light	23
This Side	25
Infant Hill, Elmwood Cemetery	27
Salvage	28
First Husband	29
Missionary	30
The Loud Family	32
Second Skin	34
The Life I Will Be Born Into	36
The Rooster	38
The Seed	40
The Landscape of My Grandmothers' Names	41
After the Miracle	43
News	45
To the Absent Wife of the Beautiful Poet at the Writers' Conference	46
Pardon	48
Afterglow	49
Ex-Brother-in-Law	51
Hello Love	53
A Definition	55
Interstate	57
Neighbors	58
Making Love to an Orphan	60
Open Swim at the Y	61

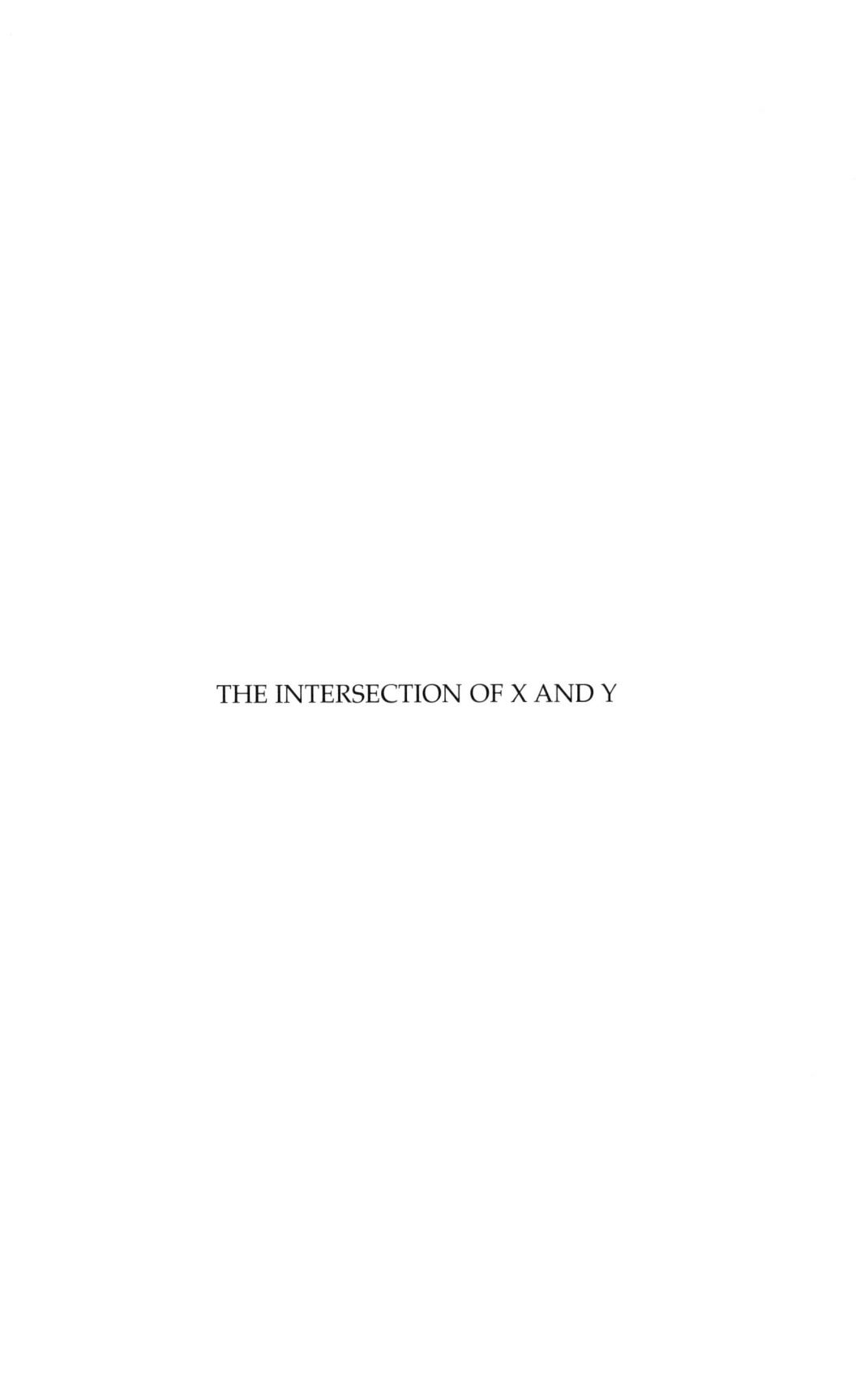

THE INTERSECTION OF X AND Y

X

Summers over tic-tac-toe I crossed out
whole afternoons, slow to see
that X marks the place where victims fall
as well as buried treasure. Years later in school

I learned a blond hair from an Iowa woman
formed the cross-sight for Hiroshima.
When I questioned my father, he nodded
slightly, sadly, and kept on plotting

the quadrants of my algebra homework,
tracing for the third time that night
the puzzling intersection of x and y. *One
chromosome,* my friend is saying. *That's all it takes.*

We are sitting outside in old-fashioned
lawn chairs that press against the backs
of our thighs, forming an intricate latticework.
Inside the house, beneath the marionette strings

of a circus mobile, her baby sleeps,
his slanted eyes and dry fissured lips
linking him to thousands of genetic brothers,
and I think of childhood Bible schools,

the missionary banner—"Christ for the World"—
stretching from the wooden pulpit
to the earth's four corners. Once I stood
in four states at once. My mother still has the photo.

There I am, seven years old, splayed like a starfish:
a hand in Colorado, another in Utah, one leg each
in Arizona and New Mexico. Around us miles
of turquoise sky where, a hundred years before,

smoke from tepees rose. *Everything
an Indian does is in a circle,* the great
Sioux chief said. *Everything tries to be round.*
Documentary cameras were clicking. He stood

inside a square reservation house and pointed
to the corners, saying *That is why we died.*
My grandfather's last month was measured
in x's of the fence he hammered

on the farthest acre of his land, while upstairs
my grandmother collected x's in her lap,
canceling the empty muslin with thread and needle,
one stitch by one stitch, until a flower bloomed.

Sidekick

This one is for Barney Fife and Barney Rubble,
for Ed and Trixie, for Ethel and Fred,
the straight man, ploy, the wooden decoy bobbing,
back-up singers with their benign doo-wops,
and the boy in the back of the choir
who is asked to just please mouth the words.
For the runner-up without whom there could be no race,
the pageant princess who will never be queen,
Miss Congeniality, the bridesmaid clutching for an instant
the white bouquet, perennial benchers suited up
in virginal uniforms, the ones off whom the light bounces,
moons to the first sun, the eclipsed girl walking the beach,
the one who packs the lunches, the one whose order
the waiter keeps forgetting, and all those casino singers
from One-Hit Hotel, spinning dizzily on the same old song,
forty five revolutions per minute for the rest of their lives.

Once I dreamed a show where no one was a star,
the cast a chorus of could-have-beens—
the envelope-opener at the Oscars, the virtuoso's
page turner, the understudy who broods each night
wingless in the wings, second-string violins, second sons,
the side of the face the camera never sees,
the big zero, placeholder, goose egg
hatching all the other numbers. First drafts, shed skin,
the flayed remains of St. Bartholomew, the chaff
and fodder, papery husks the poem wriggles out of,
the scaffolding, first skeleton dismantled,
pencil sketches, gesture studies, the armature and cantilever
supporting the ubiquitous clay, plaster molds
wasted in the service of the bronze, the slave buried
alive with her king, the discarded placenta—
first nourisher, first to go—first wives who train
their husbands to be husbands for second wives.
Exhausted breath trailing the departing car.

There are blue back roads we will never travel, slender
capillaries feeding the big red vein that feeds the heart,
unvarnished undersides of desks that will never know
the tender violence of our graffiti. Folds of skin
untouched by sun or hand, also the undiscovered pearl,
the veiled beauty, the hidden knees of nuns
who bare themselves only on the flip side of dream
in that one brief encore, the curtain call
uncalled for until now when suddenly the silence
of one hand clapping is multiplied by thousands
of one-hands-clapping, calling all the sidekicks
back to the stage—the frame bursting its picture,
torn envelopes healing themselves, the sealing wax
once broken for the words inside, now sealing
a love letter to itself, the echo in the valley
composing its first song, Peter Pan's shadow peeling free,
Bartholomew's recovered body-stocking zipping itself
back together, topped by all the hats Rembrandt painted over
in his search to find himself, while below
those hordes of idle shoes recovered from the closets
of amputees are kicking up their smooth black heels.

Traveling

When the Egyptians packed their dead,
the brain was first to go, pulled
with tweezers through the nose.
Then a slit in the side and the rest
poured out, the soft parts they tamped
separately into Canopic jars
or simply bandaged and stuffed back in
like giblets I rummage from the cavity
of the baking hen and present
to my cat, who slurps the juicy heart,
and in this I stray one step
from the Egyptians, who kept
the heart intact for the crossing
to the land of the dead, where
it would be weighed in the balance
pan, opposite Truth, which was a feather.
And any heart that tipped the scales
was eaten by Amemait the Devourer.

My husband refuses to sign the line
giving it all up. *Call it my last
selfish act*, he says, *but I'm keeping
my goddamn eyes.* I'm a card-carrying donor.
I've checked the blanks. Eyes. Kidneys.
Liver. Spleen. I'm holding off on the heart.
If I die this morning, by noon my parts
will be floating, not in Canopic urns
but more like the Mason jars lining the cellar,
beets and cucumbers swimming in brine.

You can't take it with you, but we try,
like the old woman in the news.
It's my whole life, she cried
as the tractor ripped through her home,
shoveling tons of garbage, seven refrigerators,

clothes, rotting food three feet high.
The excavation crew wore masks
to escape the air she slept in.

My grandmother swept up after herself
leaving nothing but a line
of grandchildren and one string of advice:
*Travel light. Take only what you can't
live without.* When Grandpa died,
she had nineteen dollars. She bought
a bus ticket and packed a suitcase,
one dress for each season.
On my overseas trip, I carried
bread and cheese and one small suitcase
filled with all the wrong things,
nothing fit for the weather.
The mummy I saw was Cleopatra,
age eleven, daughter of Candace,
who took with her a wooden comb,
a string of berries, a floral leaf.
Something for vanity, something for hunger,
something for memory's sake.
When my aunt died, we picked through
the rubble. Bundles of birthday cards,
widowed buttons, scarves, napkins pressed
flat in the backs of drawers.
Finally it took a bonfire.
And the things we couldn't live without
fit easily into a hamper.

Her Nakedness

At the market I see a beautiful woman—
her gray hair long and untamed, her only adornment
a three-tiered necklace of lines. The skin on her hands
is tissue-thin, dappled with sun spots,
and her voice opening on "hello" is ripe,
slightly bruised at the edges like the peaches
she places in a basket. She moves slowly
through the aisles, considering what not to buy.
I follow closely, pushing my loaded cart
and trying to imagine needing so little, year by year
learning what to step out of. First, these high heels,
rickety stairs on which I topple. I'll exchange them
for cushioned oxfords that breathe something back,
or open sandals like the ones the beautiful woman wears.
At home, I unpeel my stockings and slide
into soft shoes, lift my long skirt
high to the mirror, practicing how it will be
when I earn enough courage. Twice this summer
I've flaunted my purple veins to people I hardly know.
I don't want to become the woman in the story
who bathed in rubber underwear, ashamed for God
to see her nakedness. *Her Nakedness,* so royal a title
for such a bald sight. My aunt, who lost
her thick black hair, wears a wig for strangers.
But at home, holding court beside a new husband
and a niece with a full crown of hair, she removes
the wig and stares into our eyes, as if daring us to love her.

Demons

> *I beheld the Angel, who stretched out his arms, embracing the flame of fire. . . . This Angel, who is now become a Devil, is my particular friend.*
> William Blake, The Marriage of Heaven and Hell

One summer even the air hurt,
and sleep was just the sharp edge
I cut myself on each night.
My only nourishment, the small bone
of pain I chewed to the marrow.
Now I know why dogs hoard theirs.
Anything grows softer, sweeter,
if worked long enough. Outside
my window, a church billboard:
The deeper you are hollowed out,
the more you can contain. I think
of the most beautiful woman I know,
who wears a scar down the side
of her face. I think of bowls,
scooped out and hungry, and Job,
God's finest vessel. Blessed are
the meek, the persecuted, the poor
on whom the richest afflictions
are squandered. And those who wear
their wounds as a sign, like the whore
whose tears wet the dust on Christ's
feet while he rebuked the righteous:
He who is forgiven little, loves little.
The women at the shelter have been loved
almost to death—raccoon eyes,
the blueprints of husbands on their arms
and thighs. Friday nights the phones
ring off the hook, the men calling.
Sunday's bruises are healing, forgiveness
fills the air. And the women always answer.

We were poor, weren't we, Mother?
I ask, trying to rewrite my childhood.
Stretching those months in the quonset hut
and erasing the four bedroom house.
Poverty: it's something I could have sunk
my teeth into. Happy art is the hardest to make.
Breughel's Tower of Babel is beautiful
and Blake's tygers of wrath
are wiser than his horses of instruction.

How silent the room of the boy's head
after the demons left—tables toppled,
empty chairs where they'd once sat,
arguing. No more late night plunges
into fire or water, no tussles
in afternoon grass. When Jesus called
Come out! the little devils split,
and the boy was once again
his father's only child. At first
the crowd thought he was dead,
he was that still. Some said they heard
a cry issuing from the wound.

It has been three years since
that summer. I sleep the sleep
of the happily dead, wake singing
golden oldies, shop for potpourri
and wooden ducks, small things to make
the house a home. I'm smooth as a tray
or a rain gutter pointed downhill.
Convex, even, puffed up with joy

and health. Suffering could spill
over me and I wouldn't collect a drop.
I've joined the lonely procession
of the cured—the leper amazed at fingers
sprouting like leaves from the bark
of his arm, the old woman bent from birth
who now walks like everyone else.
I think of the boy alone in his bed,
making room for the demons and trying
to dream them back. No wonder
after the transplant, the blind man
tried to scratch out his new eyes.
Suddenly the bright world blinked
and blinked, until he learned what lids can do,
and pulled them down like shades
and swam back to the darkness he knew.

The Angle of Shadow, the Angle of Light

The hall where they are kept is a broken
wing off the main building, and in the last desk
a boy named Achilles is back
from a battle with the school psychologist,
who put him in Time Out for pissing
in a sink and beating his head
against a chalkboard until it bled.
I am the visiting poet. This is the class
of special students I have been warned against.
Last night I read an artist's notebook:
The angle of shadow must be equal
to the angle of light, so this morning
in my bag of kaleidoscopes and prisms
and peacock feathers, I packed a hard black
stone and the sun-bleached skull of a cow.

Achilles: his name tag is my cue. *A hero*
from a famous book, I say. *The greatest*
warrior of all. But the boy is shaking
his head, he's heard this before,
and he's ready with a sneer—*My name's*
from a cartoon. Later in the teachers' lounge
I learn he has been dipped in the river
more than once. His mother is gone,
he has gonorrhea of the mouth from his father,
and now when he draws a self-portrait
he sketches in fangs and fur
on the palms of his hands. *When I touch him*
he flinches, the teacher says.

The first Achilles had a caretaker, a centaur
who fed him lion entrails and the marrow
bones of bears to give him courage,
but what can I give this boy?
What do I know of battles?

My hardest fight is trying to raise
a ruckus between pen and paper, limping
backhand into morning. If words were enough,
I would trace them on bread and give him
a bite. Or like the ancient mystic,
outline them in sand, and we would
lick up the ones that would save us.

I want to believe what the Greeks believed,
that in the beginning, the unbroken
dark, a tiny seed slumbered,
and when night coupled with death,
she hatched an egg and named it Light.
It is said that in the midst of battle
the sun blazed from Achilles' head
and his shout was brighter than trumpets.
But finally nothing could save him.
Not the shield fashioned by Hephaestus,
god of fire, the greaves and helmet
forged in darkness and laid at Achilles' feet.
Not even his cry, although it reached
his mother, lost in the caves
of the sea and immortally helpless.

This Side

Early on, your passion was The Nude,
your paintings a delight of flesh
gone to flesh, the sag and droop
of gravity seducing our bodies back
to earth. *It's flesh we are drawn to,
drawn from,* you said. The last time
I saw your son alive, he was fourteen
and already you were moving
past the canvases of skin and substance.
I want to see through *this world,*
you said, *and it makes me tired.*

"The roar on the other side of silence,"
one artist called this place, warning
that we could die from it, from seeing
the grass grow, hearing the squirrel's
heart beat. In your new paintings
secret folds unfolded, crevices turned
inside out. An Ohio cornfield relinquished
its still life to the rumble between the stalks
until your own ears turned inward
and you heard the yellow silks
whispering a rumor of rain. Somewhere
on the undersides of leaves, your son
was lost, the only link a long-distance
connection once a month or so
when he called begging for the money
that would rock him into some other world.
When he quietly let go of himself
three days before Easter, you agreed
to cremation, watching the smoke
and believing that if the water stayed
still enough, the ashes you scattered

like seeds might one day sprout.
But lost is one thing. Gone, another.
I wish I'd taken a picture of his body,
you say, surprised that what you miss
is not what lies on the other side.
Yesterday for the first time in weeks
your stomach betrayed you with hunger
and you were angry that your body
was moving so soon back. You stood
in the kitchen, his clothes laid out
on the ironing board where you sifted
through them, the weekly duty
any mother might perform, pulling
from her son's dungarees the leavings
of a school day—nothing much, a few coins,
a wad of lint, a love note folded
and creased so many times it has grown
small and hard enough to be a weapon
that aimed just right and thrown with enough
velocity, might put someone's eye out.

Infant Hill, Elmwood Cemetery

In the cartography of grown-up plots, six feet
the measure of a man, it is difficult to fit
a playpen fence, expensive to mow the uneven spaces
between. So on this hillside between public housing's
dusty porches and the interstate, the babies
are planted together. A truck rumbles past,
bequeathing to the asphalt slab the wrappings
of a tire outlasting its second chance.
On the fence, honeysuckle and wild roses
entangle in the perennial lust of summer,
and a young girl walks the frontage road alone,
her hand resting on a white shirt shrouding
a belly that has swelled beyond expectation.
It is always a surprise, the seed that sprouts.
Always a surprise to bury an infant. What we mourn
is a heart that had barely stuttered, a blossoming
petal of lung, yet we must name him someone,
if only *Infant Son of Sharon and Tim.* This is enough.
Any more might sink the memory deep as these stones
promising too much: *John Fitzgerald, Malcolm,*
George Washington Carver the Fourth.
The newer graves are a comfort, soap opera's
brief bubble—*Tiffany, Brittany, Jeremy, Hope,*
names interchangeable as this row of identical
stone lambs grazing atop graves weedy with forgetfulness.
And here is a death too fresh for a marker, except
a profusion of blue carnations and a day-old helium balloon
with a few breaths left, an exhausted valentine
someone stood in line at the grocery store to buy.

Salvage

for a dead sister

I wore the bonnet knitted for you,
the hooded gown, your diapers
still folded on the dresser. Congenital,
the grown-ups said when I finally asked:
it was your heart that undid you.
The world you left, I used sparingly.
I crumbled soap slivers into the washcloth,
dug with a toothpick the last smear
of lipstick. Forty years ago and still I haunt
the aisles of secondhand stores, past
bins of blouses, trousers torn and mended,
shelves of pointed pumps I squeeze
my feet into. Here, a stone dug in
too long. A run-down heel. And hobble
in some stranger's shoes home
where my husband—who came complete
with ex-wife and son—waits for me,
his face softening like a leather glove
worn just long enough. Dinnertime,
I pull from the bureau an old quilt
and spread it across the table.
Now where someone's feet
once rested, there is this plate.

First Husband

After the marriage exploded, it sifted
down to this: the scar your fist left
on the filing cabinet where I kept my poems,
and on the ironing board stacks of Army khakis
whose pleats never flattened to your satisfaction.
It helped to think of you that way, a detonation
searing my eyes from everything but the white flash
that lit my path years later to a place
where I was still young enough to pass
as a bride. I've kept you hidden, even my friends
don't know. And I had almost buried you
when the Christmas card came—your fourth wedding,
complete with children acquired along the way.
Your chest has dropped, and gone completely
is the hairline that began its early retreat
when you were still the boy I would marry.
Your shirt is wrinkled; beside you
the new wife is already starting to fade.
Something in her chin reminds me of me. I send
my best wishes. For finally after twenty years
a memory ripens and falls into my lap:
our last trip, a Canadian forest
where strange animals destined for extinction
roamed the green hills. At a roadside stand
we stopped for melons. Later you steered
with one hand, and all the way down the mountain
I licked the sweetness from your fingers.

Missionary

Not the position you take with a man,
but the real calling you first hear
over ocean waters or sitting in church
and before you know it you're bringing home strays.
At five, Alice LaConte from the apartments,
her lice hitchhiking in your hair. All night
your mother scrubs, muttering, *Your friends, honey,
your friends*, but the zeal is just beginning
and by first grade you're bringing them for dinner,
their scabs and ticks and ringworm
infecting the whole family, so for weeks
you must all drink black syrup and change
underwear three times a day. In junior high
it's Melinda with the limp, first time up
you choose her for your tennis partner
and thank her for the opportunity. In high school,
it's *you* he loves, Bo Pederson
with the stuttering eye reflecting the ghosts
of the parents he stabbed, but you see only
the bright flower of his need, so of course
in college it's the broken one you want,
the hood who has slept six nights
in his jacket, your first date is to the bank
where you withdraw prematurely your entire
savings to pay for some brown-eyed girl's abortion,
so that night he sits across a booth from you
and writes a rhyming poem about a blue-eyed
saint who loves him in spite of, and because
that's what you've been training for,
by June you're kneeling at the altar
(as close to China as you'll ever get) and finally in bed
when you take the missionary position,
it's an orgy, it's the whole unwashed mob you love,
sure you will sustain them forever so you're astonished
to wake and find them gone without a thank-you,

him and that multitude of sinners
you've been courting all these years.

The Loud Family

Across the empty space of these hills,
it's hard to keep secrets from your neighbors,
especially in summer, windows open
to the bullfrog's swampy bellow, the racket
of birds whose names we don't know.
My husband and I are city people who own
a piece of this place, and until last year
our neighbors were a splash of local color,
laughable as a cartoon family. We named them
the Louds—the father, all paunch and swagger,
a hunting rifle over his shoulder,
two small boys running behind him calling,
"Deddy, can we go? Can we?" And the retriever,
having recently emptied another round
of puppies onto the dirt floor of her pen,
would trot the road between our houses,
her teats sloshing wildly. The Loud mother,
a baby girl slung across her hip, waved
from the second-floor porch where she stood
gazing at the satellite dish as if it were
some giant moon, her voice scraping
against the evening, a sea chantey
turned lullaby. Nights after supper the only
light from their house was a blue flicker,
then that blasted metallic clamor—
can after can of sitcom laughter
opening at the windows of our cabin
where we sat caressing the slim necks
of Chardonnay glasses, or quietly
turning pages of biography and poetry,
entering the lives of those whose daily grunts
and wheezes had been distilled
into something finer, the way I sometimes
make love to my husband, trying not to let
my body get in the way, trying not to be

the way I once imagined the Louds, their bellies
slapping noisily together. So I was shocked
when a neighbor delivered the news:
the younger son had stepped on a sewing needle,
and his blood poisoned swiftly. I'd never
thought of death and the Louds together,
could not have guessed how fine a suture
grief would stitch, how heavy the silence
that traveled the valley between us.
A year has passed, it's summer again,
and we've opened the windows. A buzz saw
shrieks, it's the father building a fence
so the little girl won't toddle too far.
Puppies are whimpering, a new baby daughter
is mewing, it's good to hear them at it again.
The mother hollers at the son who is left,
and I can tell by his whine he's happy
to be yelled at. Beneath the shadow
of the satellite dish, the retriever lifts her head
as if trying to trace a rustle in the grass, then
returns to her brood, licking their sealed eyes.

Second Skin

for the infant sister who died the year I was born

Dost thou know who made thee?
. . .
Gave thee clothing of delight,
Softest clothing wooly bright.
         William Blake, "The Lamb"

Yes I know whose pelt I wore
those first few hours,
whose woolly death covered me,
a sheep in sheep's clothing—

for I've seen an orphan
at lambing time, tottering
in a borrowed cloak,
suck the teat

of a dead lamb's mother.
My shepherd friend tells me
how this trick is turned:
with a knife he unzips

the carcass of the dead lamb
which peels off in one piece,
tail and all, even the sack
of each slippered foot,

all the way to the muzzle
and the twin leaves of ears,
a perfect body stocking
which fits neatly over

the orphaned lamb
who, now doubly warmed,
twice blest, wobbles on new legs
across the blood-dried straw

where the mother waits,
her womb still slack
from its recent emptying.
The miracle, my friend says,

is how easily she takes
the lost one for her own.
A quick sniff, a nuzzle,
and the milk ducts answer,

while the lamb, already
itching to shed the jacket
of the dead, fastens itself
to the rubbery teat

and the mother gives in,
her black eyes staring
dumbly at the burial field
pocked with stones.

The Life I Will Be Born Into

My father is feeding the wood stove its breakfast
of poplar and oak, rousing the drowsy cinders.
My sister and brother are asleep in feather beds,
the warming bricks at their feet now cold
as the headstone one baby sister sleeps beneath.
They are too young to understand where she has gone
or to notice the possibility under their mother's gown.
I hiccup and make my first fist. Mother is a heartbeat
and warm waters rolling over the life I will become,
a child so hungry for stories I will rob
even this moment, this morning that is their lives.
The well is dry, the field a stubble of blunted crops,
but my mother trusts what morning will offer.
She latches rubber waders at her thighs and throws
a fishing basket over her shoulder. A cane pole
is her walking stick. The path to Wildcat is ragged
and steep and she weaves between oak roots
that years later will trip me. I ride the waters
of her strength and toss my first tale from the future
into her past: the woman in the creek
is younger than the mother I will remember.
Her hips are wide, the boots planted decisively
on the creek bed. Ripples of water, learning
the borders of her body, thread their way around her.

Now the basket is alive with trout and she hauls
herself into the clearing, water rushing from the pockets
of her trousers: she had gone deeper than she had planned.
She pushes through a tangle of vine, begins the long
climb up the hill, her breath coming in quick hard pants,
a labor punctuated by the whoosh of the pole
brushing against leaves. Had there been an easier path,
she might have taken it. At the house she unloads herself
onto the back steps, empties the waders and squeezes
from her trousers the last drops of Wildcat Creek.

The white paint on the farmhouse is peeling, the porch
mud-speckled from the snouts of piglets that soon
will escape and slurp the poison meant for the fox
who has been slashing the chickens' bellies. But for now
there is this offering and the new sun approves,
sprinkles bits of light through her black hair,
across the flannel jacket. The first trout floats
from the bucket to her hand and she slits it
with a kitchen knife, tossing the entrails to the pink sow
rooting nearby. Within minutes my brother and sister,
eyes crusted with sleep, will be warming their hands
over the wood stove, and my mother will dust the trout
with flour and drop it deep in crackling grease.

The Rooster

Bad boy. Last night he jerked the I.V. from his arm
and escaped from his bed where it took
three nurses to strap him down,
this shriveled bantam, ninety-six pounds
of gut and gristle, a pound for each year.

In the school picture, my grandfather is third
from the left, eyes squeezed against the flash, fists
balled tight and ready. His first memory
is catching a stove-pipe as it fell
into his baby buggy behind the kitchen stove.
At three he walked too close to a woodcutter
and was struck by the pole of an ax. At six
a horse knocked him breathless. Once,
lost in the woods, he lived on frozen apples,
hunted skunk and fox and early learned
the unearthly cry of a mink close at hand.
At twelve, his mother died. He remembers
how his father and sister crawled
into his narrow bed. Morning found them
huddled like chicks until he stood and brushed
himself off, shook his father's scent
from his sleeve and strutted to work.
Corn picker. Feed store clerk. Factory worker.
Pool room shark. Carpenter. Inspector.
Salesman. Farmer. He once told me
he was so poor it hurt, but he was never broke.

Now he is telling stories, his voice gravel
over gravel. This one is from childhood,
about a dog tied in a sack with rocks
and thrown into the river. The sack loosened,
he surfaced and lived a long, ferocious life.
He recalls the dog's name, Pedro, but cannot
call mine, although he says the eyes look familiar.

His are rheumy, shrouded in a caul. And now
he's onto his favorite story: himself.
Cock of the walk, strutting all his lives
before me. Last year he wrote it, sold
hardback copies to strangers in banks and buses.
Mean as a roll of barb wire, he tells it. *Tough
as a piece of whang.* That's how he made
the bell ring! Fifteen hundred pounds
on the striking machine, and left-handed, too!
Around him the big men gathered.
Calling him Shorty cost one man
new plow shoes smack in the mouth.

At dawn he finally nods in mid-tale. I lay
my head on the bed, smelling his sweat
like creek water backed up too long.
He stirs and mumbles. The hospital gown
has ridden to his navel, past the place
where it began, the seed that grew
my mother, then passed to me.
When I reach to untangle the gown, I see
what is left, the fallen flesh
pulled free from muscle, the papery skin.
Then he calls out, as if to split the daylight
open, *We shouldn't have killed
the rooster and eaten him!* and whether
he is dreaming or remembering, I cannot know.

The Seed

Mother's belly that summer
was huge and creaseless
and the doll she gave me
was rubbery slick, its skin
stretched tight over stubborn
legs that would not bend
and sausage arms stiff
in their casings. I had seen
missionary posters of children
swollen with hunger
and on our street a dead
dog engorged with August.
Maybe death was like a seed.
Maybe it was planted in Mother
and every night it would tick
and tick until finally it puffed her up
like the blowfish in the encyclopedia.
In the bedroom above me,
Mother slept, the baby inside
still faceless as a party balloon
growing from someone's
puckered lips, while I lay
under covers with my doll, stroking
the eyes that would not close,
the swollen pellet toes.

The Landscape of My Grandmothers' Names

for Golda Groves and Sylvia Mounts

Silver and gold rings worn thin on knotted
roots of their fingers. Between them
a century of married nights, starched gowns
and the everpresent slop jar beside the bed.
In the east window, heat lightning is building,
then suddenly the flash, gray sky releasing
its earned metallic anger like the taste of blood
in my grandmother's mouth that summer
decades before I was born, the single gold filling
she dug from a tooth and redeemed
for flour and lard. Or like rust on my lips
from the morning's first dipper of well water
pumped by a grandmother's arm.
When I dream them it is always summer.
The smell of sweat and the yeasty rise
of bread in metal pans. I stand between them,
cool and safe in the shade of their lives.
For them, only flat and flatter fields,
soybeans and corn, row upon row,
perfectly even, white sun bleaching
the wide spaces between. No grove to hide in,
no mountain from which to view
the scene from higher ground. One grandmother
climbed a stallion, rode out her fears
on his back. The other cooled her rage
in icy creeks, hip-deep in minnows.

From eaves and gutters the rainwater trickled
into barrels to be collected for the Saturday
rinsing of daughters' hair, eight daughters
between them, not counting the ones
marked by hand-carved stones. Not counting
granddaughters, or great, that keep coming

years past my grandmothers' deaths
entangling like vines into one large death
and all the details confused. Golda laughed
her last words to a daughter who lifted her
from the bed. *Look what earth does to us!*
she said, meaning what was left
of her flesh as it spilled over the bedpan.
Sylvia was silent at the end, hands folded
across her breasts, still beautiful even at ninety.

In the only picture of them together
they are standing on a makeshift airfield
on either side of my pilot father who guides
an elbow of each. *Mother,* he called one. *Mom,*
the other, and this flight is a gift, their first
and last time *up*. Their housedresses are fluttering
around their knees, chiffon scarves tied
over their tarnished hair. Behind them
the propeller spins its dangerous circle.
Soon both will laugh at how quickly—considering
their combined weights—the plane lifts
from the ground. Both will look down
without fear, surprised to see how small
everything is, how well their lives continue
without them: the fields and plow horse,
tiny dots of grandchildren emerging
from the barn, the stream only this morning
engorged with rain and the promise of trout,
now a thin ribbon, insignificant as the loose
thread a child discovers and pulls and pulls,
amazed at how easily it all comes undone.

After the Miracle

Maybe he had just settled
into his best sleep in years,
the winding sheets wrapped snug, dust
clustering around his eyes. Perhaps in death
he finally smiled, knowing that outside
his tomb, two women loved him more
than ever and Jesus himself was weeping.
Then the voice: *Lazarus, come forth!*
What could he do? Of course he was flattered.
It wasn't easy, bound hand and foot,
but he stumbled out, four days dead
and stinking. It would be months before
he knew the truth: coming back
is the easy part. Even Jesus didn't press
his luck, his second time back
a brief appearance, then just as suddenly,
gone! The apostles gasped, staring
at the hole in the sky. Not so for Lazarus.
At home he sinks into the doldrums
of health and his accustomed evening chair.
Mary yawns and stirs the pottage
as he talks to her back, the same story.
And every morning, Martha grabs the broom,
grumbling at the mess he made—the twisted
bedclothes on the cot, the ordinary dust.

Two thousand years later I emerge
blinking, fresh from a miracle of my own.
I roll the cart through grocery aisles and weep
at the perfection of onions. *Life is a blessing!*
I sing to the bag boy, tipping him
five dollars as if he were responsible.
At the bank the teller's *How are you?*
crackles through speakers of the drive-through
window. *I'm alive!* I shout to the pneumatic tube

that sucks my paycheck miraculously
into her hands. I was pulled through the tunnel
and back. What else matters? For weeks
I thank everyone and pay my bills
as soon as they drop through the slot.
I give to charity. The green faces
of presidents wink back, a conspiracy of joy.
For days I walk this delicate crust. Just like
the movies. Then in the distance I hear
the chorus of the lost, humming
as if they missed me. The disposal backs up
once too often and Wednesdays begin
to fold in like hospital corners on a sheet.

News

for a sister

It is March, mud weather,
and the worms have left signatures,
castings of their former selves.
Your sons are outside turning
over rocks, searching the chaos
of kingdom and phylum for some
small order—a slug or centipede
bristling with life. I join them,
eager to trace in this changing
calligraphy some further mention
of spring. Yesterday the cancer
tests came back and tomorrow
the sac that grew these children
will be clamped and pulled out.
And you will lie in white forgetfulness
while the pathologist reads your cells'
possible futures. But in this moment
you are here, sweeping the porch.
Helicopter leaves circle your head,
husks carried by the wind.
The younger son shovels a universe
of soil into a bucket while the oldest
smears dirt across his temple,
a primitive marking. Below our feet
whole worlds go on without us
and everything tapers down to a dark
burrowing, like the common worm,
Lumbricus terrestris, who makes its way
by swallowing the earth, which is
its chief obstacle. Inch by blind inch
it thrusts its blunt head forward,
pulsing with blood and carrying
more hearts than it will ever use.

*To the Absent Wife of the Beautiful Poet
    at the Writers' Conference*

I want you to know that nothing happened,
and everything that might have is now sewn
into the hoop of Arizona sky
that stretched above our heads that shy
evening of talk when we left our books
and went out to read the papery news
of bougainvillea. Here was vegetation
more animal than plant, the dangerous spine
of cactus, its fleshy stem and thistle,
and those rubbery tongues lolling speechless
in the desert air where even domestic
herbs turn wild, parsley and dill spilling
over their planned containers. When your husband
broke off a piece of rosemary and held it
out to me, I smelled the sharp clean scent
of marriage, the scent that fills my loved world
three time zones away. My garden, the spotted
cat and aged brandy, the bed pillow minted
with the imprint of my husband's head.
Yet I confess that part of me wanted
to take in that moment the man you more
than half-made, knowing that what I love
most in married men is what is given
by wives. The elbow he leans upon
is your elbow, his listening quiet,
your quiet, practiced in twenty years
of bedtime conversation. If he loved,
in that instant, anything in me, it was
the shape and smell of one whole woman
made from the better halves of two—
your hard earned past and my present, briefly
flaming. Not long ago I watched a girl
I might have been twenty years ago, sit
literally at my husband's feet and adore him.

There are gifts we can give our husbands,
but adoration is not one. If I could,
I would be one woman diverging, walk
one road toward those things that matter
always, the trail long love requires.
The other, for what burned in the eyes
of your husband as he asked, *What is the secret
to a long marriage?* I gave my grandfather's
bald reply: *You don't leave and you don't die.*
There are no secrets. Together, the four of us—
your husband, mine, you and I,
have lasted. I started to say forty
married years, but no, it is eighty,
each of us living those years sometimes,
by necessity, singly, the whole of love
greater than the sum of its combined hearts.
That's what I mean about the sky. Its blueness
and the way it goes on forever. An old
teacher told me if you break a line in half
again and again, you will never reach an end.
Infinity is measured by the broken spaces
within as well as by the line spooling out
as far as we can see. I love my husband.
Still, there were spaces in that evening
that will go on dividing our lives. And if
the sky had not begun in that moment
to blink messages of light from stars I thought
had died out long ago, I might have answered
your husband's eyes another way.
And there would have been heaven to pay.

Pardon

May I be excused? I ask from the breakfast table
and Mother scans my plate. The clock
above my head sweeps its black hand,
but nothing is cleaner. Outside on the street
my friends plod their Saturday road to confession.
So much to haul, and I too want to spill it
to the deep voice behind the curtain
while Mother Mary looks on, condoning again
for one more week, my entire plate of sin.
But I am Baptist. My salvation, one public wringing
that had to take, the choir singing "Just As I Am,"
as I ask *May I be excused?* to Jesus,
who lifts his dying head, the crown of thorns,
and nods just once before his last words,
and I carry that nod the rest of my days,
like the wilted lunch bag I fold and bring home
each day to Mother. Years later
in the back seats of cars when the warm tongues of boys
lap up the memory of that ancient forgiveness,
I see them again, my Catholic friends
floating back from confession, the accordion
pleats on their skirts like a sheaf of new leaves
turning over, their patent leather shoes
immaculate, the sun on their backs like a pardon.

Afterglow

>*for my first husband*

When you left our new marriage for another woman's bed,
the sheets were still rumpled from unfinished loving.
I didn't know it would be our last try. Twenty years
since I've seen you, but lately I've been replaying the scene,
and since only in bed did we ever agree (and even then, clumsily)
I keep tucking us in, wishing to dream it right:
a one night, last chance reunion, the decades of dammed-up
guilt and regret pushing against our bodies until—
as they say in romance novels—we are flooded with passion.

When the dam finally breaks and the dream trickles through
we're back in your teenage bedroom. The same fringed lamp,
the polished row of debate trophies, the chenille spread
your mother washed and fluffed each Saturday.
At the foot of the bed she's still fluffing,
and from the champagne bottle on the nightstand
your father effervesces, his head the cork popping.
Remember at the engagement party how he lifted his glass,
a toast of warning: *If you wonder how your wife*
will look in twenty years, just look at her mother.
Well darling, here I am. You, too, across the room of this dream,
wearing your father's timid hairline, his paunch blooming
over your belt buckle as you move to unlatch it.
Your parents fizzle as bubbles do, and we are left
surveying each other, our expressions forgiving, and more:
pride in the wisdom of early choices. *You look good,*
you've held up well, we say. *I always knew you would.*

The rest is coda. The bed, an appointment we must keep.
I would not name it passion. Perhaps it is the only gift
we know to give or take. We unwrap it the best we can,
coaxing out moans and when it is over, exhausted thanks.
What a relief to have it finished—the failures, the burden

that memory lays on us, the expectation of lust.
Just to lie here mildly amused, after all these years
finally postcoital. Grateful it was nothing, really.
Glad not to wake with my little finger
in my mouth, wet, still dreamy, wishing you back.

Ex-Brother-in-Law

Without the law, there is no brother,
and no ceremony to mark the breaking.
Christmas Eve from the box packed away last year
we uncover the stocking stitched with your name,
not knowing what to do with it. Later as we gather
to watch family slides projected on a sheet,
your face surfaces among ours, miraculous
as the imprints emerging on the shroud of Turin.
When you were here, how simple it seemed,
the pattern of blame and solution: if only you would turn
that way or this, if only you would disappear,
my sister's life could begin again. But what of *our* lives,
the severed sisters, aunts, brothers, nephews, nieces,
fathers, mothers—all those unregistered
couplings of hearts—left to wonder
if you were ever ours, and by what decree.

Have you married some new family, are you sharing
their holiday feast while we sit here
at the table you refinished—your windburnt hands
with the freckled knuckles, rough-hewn hands
that sanded until the grain revealed itself,
the complicated whorls beneath the surface
where so much of you remains. The daughter
you started fourteen years ago wears your face
and keeps growing. And your son still brags
about the time you accidentally shot a power-driven
nail through your hand while building
a skate ramp—*For me!* he sings proudly. *For me!*

It's the small things that make a job,
you once said as you knelt eye-level to the task:
this cabinet you built to store the mementos,
all the odd, unmatched relics that have no place.
You worked two days and we were satisfied.

No, you said, *it's the finishing that matters.*
Another day's labor found its completion:
a hand sanded notch and this perfectly engineered
sliding latch with its effortless closing and opening.

Hello Love

She has sent these words into the future
to no one in particular. I find them
in next month's calendar planted on her desk.
My niece's handwriting loops back
on itself, each vowel so womanly
in its roundness, the o's might be eggs
or breasts, or the flower of an open mouth.
She has written *love,* not *lover,*
addressing the whole world of possibility.
No comma separates the greeting
from the greeted: it is hello love she wants.
Her father is huge in his chosen absence,
growing larger each year she waits.

Not long ago, temporarily lost
between the goodbye and hello of a man
I had loved since before she was born,
I drove my niece up a mountain. I thought
it was time she saw the view, how small
our city from this height, how the shoulders
of the most impressive hills soften
when draped with fog. *It's okay,* she said.
Don't worry, he'll be back. On the way down
an approaching truck swerved, its drunken
headlights swimming, and I slammed my arm
across her chest—a mother's gesture,
inherited and useless—as if the laws of physics
alter for those we love. No matter this time.
We escaped with our lives, all our pasts
and futures hurtling toward us. At sixteen,
my hair like hers was long and heavy,
a luxurious burden I carried for love.
And when the boy left for no reason,
I sliced off the hair and hid in my room,
a Rapunzel with no means of escape.

My father, home from Vietnam,
knocked and entered, his eyes downcast
as if he were the one responsible.
I expected to hear *We love you,*
the knot of words he kept in his throat
and untied in times like these.
Instead, he gave the difficult pronoun,
claiming me as his own. My answer
was to turn and throw myself onto the bed.
In that moment I would have traded
seven fathers for the boy who was gone.
What I meant to say to my niece
as the valley beneath us dissolved in mist
was that *hello* almost never spells *love.*
There is room in the hollows of *goodbye*
for a full-grown woman to hide.
The first man who left me was not my father.
Yet still I fall again and again in love
with the backs of men. And it will be a long time
before the face opening toward her
is more beautiful than the one turning away.

A Definition

Love, you once told me,
means you could give your wife
an enema if it came to that.
You say the sweetest things, I thought.
I was young and childless and could not
imagine allowing anyone that much access.
When we met, you were already a father.
I married you partly for that. My mother
always said every man wants a son,
and yours was so conveniently there,
courtesy of a first wife I knew only
through the signature on the backs
of child support checks. Tonight
we talk of your mother's cancer
which once in a letter I misread as *career*,
and it might as well have been,
she gave so much to it. Now that it is done,
it is not the memory of her pain
that breaks you, but the unnatural tilt of the wig
and the sound of your old bicycle horn
which she retrieved from the attic
and carried with her to the bathroom
so your father could hear
if she got stranded, the way a wild gander
hears the distant honk of his mate
and swoops down to answer.

Last night after an expensive dinner
we made anniversary love
in a bed so crowded with years
I once told you I don't want to know
who else is in here with us,
all the lives and loves confused.
Hours later, the veal turned to poison,
sweat slid off my nakedness

as I shivered in the bathroom—
my head in the waste can—and called out,
amazed to see you suddenly there,
naked in the blue fluorescence.
Then, in some remembered gesture,
you placed a washcloth on my forehead.
When I was finally emptied, I looked up
into the mirror, saw our future,
your father hurrying through the door:
then *one of us* holding *one of us*.

Interstate

In the back seat my newly orphaned mother
is sleeping off her father. I am driving her home
for the funeral. Since Grandmother's death ten years ago
I've waited for the other shoe to fall, and now finally
the thunk eight hundred miles away. It's just like him
to die like this, to spoil my mother's vacation. Hundreds
of times he could have slipped away in her arms,
the arms that lifted him, fed him, put him to bed.
He could have died with a blessing on his lips,
was that too much to ask? A truck passes.
I watch the yellow dotted line, a tenuous perforation.

Now she is up, her face creased from the ribbed
upholstery. My eyes in the rearview mirror mirror hers,
crinkle around the lids. *The minute someone dies,
you begin to forget*, she says. *It's hard to hold
anything against him.* And the tears she thought impossible
slip down her face. We pass Tennessee farmhouses,
all the dresses he refused his daughters
snapping on strangers' lines. Then on into Kentucky
where his infidelities limp like wounded dogs
into the mountains. We roll toward Indiana
and I remember the last time I saw him, toothless
and diapered, whimpering for his mother who died
when he was twelve. Someone has planted poppies
in the median. The odometer clicks, turns over a new
thousand, rows of zeros adding up to nothing,
and three hours later when we cross the state line,
we're laughing at his joke about the farmer
and the cow. Mile by mile we relinquish the road.

Neighbors

Last night while we slept the sound
sleep of the long married,
the couple next door moved out,
leaving the remnants of their quarrel
strewn beside the curb for the morning
pick-up: broken slats from a director's chair,
a few old albums, some cardboard boxes
I was tempted to open. When they moved in—
two young men—they planted
a garden which spread out of all logic,
as if some horticultural secret
were buried in the soil. Their garden grew
bloodroot, stepbrother to Sweet William.
Purple coleus with corduroy leaves,
impatiens sprouting glorious pinks and corals.
July mornings while I bent in the heat
to pinch back the chrysanthemum's
premature bloom, the lovers lounged
in silk pajamas on a sofa they'd carried
to the porch, plumped with cushions.
Music, old enough to mean something,
crackled from a phonograph whose cord
snaked through an open window.
I paused on my knees to listen, recalling
the face and hands of a man I briefly loved.
When October turned over its old leaf,
my mums opened on schedule
their tight fists, while next door
tall stems, grown too fragile
to support the heavy heads of bloom,
bowed over grass littered with leaves.
The neighbors took the dog, but left
the chain rusting on a wooden deck
whose gaps are now packed with acorns
and seeds. They took the fountain

in the shape of a boy balanced precariously
on one perfect foot. Between us we shared
a brick wall, an alley that accessed
our back gates, and the generous trunk
of a hackberry tree whose limbs
reached into our separate yards.
They left a birdbath open to the sky.
If someone doesn't turn it to the ground,
come January it will glaze over
with a brilliant silver sheen
and crack in the first hard freeze.

Making Love to an Orphan

I've heard of men who suddenly
don't know how to touch their wives
once the wives become mothers,
the familiar body now a foreign land
they have no right to enter.
Since we buried your mother
our bed is a small boat rocking
toward a port of strange customs.
My sisters wave from the shore.
They arrived years ago, having
married lost boys motherless
from the start. My sisters are not afraid
of growing large and soft, of becoming
the country their husbands and children
bury themselves in. But I chose instead
to marry a *man*, and now look
at this boy in my arms. Here are bones
I've never felt before. I don't know
how to hold him or what to say,
my tongue and hands mute,
no coin to spend, no language
for this difficult crossing.

Open Swim at the Y

Capped and goggled, I begin my crawl
with the other turtles at the shallow end.
Sometimes a winner crowns the waves,
like the muscled lifeguard who churns air to water,
water to air, in the perfect butterfly. But mostly
we are learners. Beside me, a hairless old man
recovers. *A stroke,* his wife whispers
as she dog-paddles to his pace. At the edge
two retarded girls who call themselves Dumbo and Jumbo
are diving for pennies as if they were pearls.
Though shallow, it is a long way down for them,
with bodies like overgrown toddlers
dragging the baggage of buttocks and breasts.
Through goggles I watch them underwater
the way I watched baby whales through the scratched
exhibit glass at Sea World when I was small
and believed all mongoloids were related, the same eyes,
slanted yet unbearably round. The same puffy face,
the same flesh collecting at the elbows and knees.
Now I am told not to call them mongoloids,
the world has renamed them, yet still the tribal name
floats to me and with it, a thirty-year memory—
how each morning as I waited alone at the stop,
their special bus would pass. Against the glass
they would press identical faces and smile,
waving their swollen hands as if to include me.
And I would turn from the love they gave so easily.
Now Jumbo taps my goggles, sticks a thumb in her ear,
wiggles her fingers. *Catch me!* she calls as she pulls
her sodden weight from the water, then, flat-footed,
slaps her way past the lifeguard. A woman dives in,
her false breast escapes and sails toward me
and I remember my aunt's mastectomy, the form
she tried so hard to fill. I rescue the breast and hand it back,
but she shrugs, tosses it onto her towel and kicks from me,

making her way. Rocked in her wake, Jumbo and Dumbo bob past, twin buoys marking a safe passage. Dumbo turns and waves, as if to seal some old contract, and I lift my hand, turn my face to the water and begin my slow crawl back.